ANCIENT WARRIORS

MĀORI
WARRIORS

KENNY ABDO

Fly!
An Imprint of Abdo Zoom
abdobooks.com

abdobooks.com

Published by Abdo Zoom, a division of ABDO, P.O. Box 398166, Minneapolis,
Minnesota 55439. Copyright © 2021 by Abdo Consulting Group, Inc. International
copyrights reserved in all countries. No part of this book may be reproduced in any
form without written permission from the publisher. Fly!™ is a trademark and logo
of Abdo Zoom.

Printed in the United States of America, North Mankato, Minnesota.
052020
092020

Photo Credits: Alamy, AP Images, Everett Collection, Getty Images, iStock,
newscom, Shutterstock, Wikimedia
Production Contributors: Kenny Abdo, Jennie Forsberg, Grace Hansen
Design Contributors: Dorothy Toth, Neil Klinepier, Laura Graphenteen

Library of Congress Control Number: 2019956155

Publisher's Cataloging-in-Publication Data

Names: Abdo, Kenny, author.
Title: Maori warriors / by Kenny Abdo
Description: Minneapolis, Minnesota : Abdo Zoom, 2021 | Series: Ancient warriors |
    Includes online resources and index.
Identifiers: ISBN 9781098221232 (lib. bdg.) | ISBN 9781098222215 (ebook) |
    ISBN 9781098222703 (Read-to-Me ebook)
Subjects: LCSH: Maori (New Zealand people)--Juvenile literature. | Maori (New Zealand
    people)--Warfare--Juvenile literature. | Maori (New Zealand people)--Social life
    and customs--Juvenile literature. | Military art and science--Juvenile literature. |
    Soldiers--Juvenile literature.
Classification: DDC 305.899442--dc23

TABLE OF CONTENTS

MĀORI WARRIORS

The Māori have earned the reputation as some of the most unforgiving, fierce warriors of the **South Seas**.

The Māori warriors come from small tribal groups. They pass down stories and strong traditions of warfare.

THE WARRIORS

The Māori people were the first humans to live in New Zealand. They traveled from another island in **Polynesia** around 1,000 years ago.

Face tattoos hold a special significance to the Māori people. The tattoos are carved into the skin using a chisel and hammer. Each line shows the person's bravery and strength.

Every Māori male was trained as a warrior from a young age. One specific thing they worked on was wrist strength. This training made their handheld weapons much more effective.

WARFARE & TACTICS

Māori warriors used spears and long clubs as weapons. They also had **mere clubs** attached to their belts for close-range fighting. They never used shields.

One tactic used by the Māori warriors was a traditional native dance. It is called the **Haka**. The dance was used to intimidate their opponents. It was also performed as a ritual before battle.

The most commonly used strategy of Māori warriors was the **ambush**. They used various tricks and disguises to attack their enemies.

The Battle of Hingakaka was the largest battle in Māori history. It happened in the late 18th century between two Māori tribes. More than 12,000 warriors perished.

The Musket Wars began in 1807. This war lasted for more than 30 years. It was the first time firearms were used by the Māori in combat. As many as 3,000 battles were fought. More than 30,000 lives were lost.

ARE YOU NOT ENTERTAINED?!

The **Haka** is used by many sports teams today. There have even been regular competitive Haka festivals between different Māori tribes since 1972.

The Māori language has made a comeback in mainstream culture. *Te reo*, which means "the language," has appeared in the hit movie *Moana* and pop songs that top the charts!

GLOSSARY

ambush – a surprise attack.

Haka – translates to "posture dance." The participants say a chant, stomp their feet, stick out their tongues, and bulge out their eyes.

mere club – a weapon shaped like a teardrop and made from bone, jade, or stone. It was the most common weapon used by the Māori.

Polynesia – a region made up of more than 1,000 islands scattered throughout the central and southern Pacific Ocean.

South Seas – commonly refers to the South Pacific, which includes places like New Zealand, Hawaii, and Samoa.

ONLINE RESOURCES

Booklinks
NONFICTION NETWORK
FREE! ONLINE NONFICTION RESOURCES

To learn more about Māori Warriors, please visit **abdobooklinks.com** or scan this QR code. These links are routinely monitored and updated to provide the most current information available.

INDEX